AF552409

GIRL
TALK

Books by

Sandra Byrd

FROM BETHANY HOUSE PUBLISHERS

Girl Talk

THE HIDDEN DIARY

Cross My Heart

Make a Wish

Just Between Friends

Take a Bow

61 QUESTIONS
From Girls Like You!

BETHANYHOUSE
MINNEAPOLIS, MN 55438

Girl Talk: 61 Questions From Girls Like You!

Cover design by Cheryl Neisen

Published by Bethany House Publishers
A Ministry of Bethany Fellowship International
11400 Hampshire Avenue South
Bloomington, Minnesota 55438
www.bethanyhouse.com

Printed in the United States of America by
Bethany Press International, Bloomington, Minnesota 55438

Library of Congress Cataloging-in-Publication Data

Byrd, Sandra.
Girl talk : 61 questions from girls like you! (with answers from the Bible) / by Sandra Byrd.
p. cm.
ISBN 0-7642-2492-1 (pbk.)
1. Girls—Religious life—Miscellanea—Juvenile literature. 2. Christian life—Biblical teaching—Miscellanea—Juvenile literature. [1. Christian life. 2. Conduct of life.] I. Title.
BV4551.3 .B97 2001
248.8'2—dc21 2001001328

SANDRA BYRD lives near beautiful Seattle, between the snow-capped Mount Rainier and the Space Needle, with her husband and two children (and let's not forget her Australian shepherd, Trudy). When she's not writing, she's usually reading, but she also likes to scrapbook, listen to music, and spend time with friends. Besides writing *Girl Talk*, she's also the author of THE HIDDEN DIARY books and the bestselling series SECRET SISTERS.

Contents

Rain and snow fall from the sky.
They don't return without watering the ground.
They cause the plants to sprout and grow.
And the plants make seeds for the farmer.
And from these seeds people have bread to eat.

The words I say do the same thing.
They will not return to me empty.
They make the things happen that I want to happen.
They succeed in doing what I send them to do.

Isaiah 55:10–11

Welcome to *Girl Talk*! I'm glad you're here!

What is *Girl Talk*?

Girl Talk is a book of questions from real life. Girls just like you wrote each and every question. Girls have problems that are real, and the Bible has answers that are real. I hope this book will help you to solve some of your real problems with great biblical solutions.

Are these the only answers from the Bible?

No. The Bible is chock-full of good things to say—thousands of pages of it! But the Bible doesn't ever disagree with itself. These are some good answers from the Bible. You'll have to keep studying it over a lifetime so you know more and more of what God has to say. He wants to talk to you every day. Every time you read the Bible you will learn something new.

How do I use this book?

You can take the quizzes at the beginning of each section to see which problems you might have that other girls do, too. You can read the answers to them. You can do one page a day, or you can do as many in a day as you want. One thing—promise me that you will *answer the questions* (with more than just a yes or no) and *do the action points* after each question. *Please!* Just reading them won't change your life, but doing them will!

How do I get started figuring out some answers?

Why, turn the page!

Faith

We live by faith, not by sight.

2 Corinthians 5:7 (NIV)

Quiz

YES NO

- ☐ ☐ **Were you ever embarrassed when you shared your faith with someone?** *See page 12.*
- ☐ ☐ **Do you ever worry if you're really saved or if you are really going to heaven?** *See page 13.*
- ☐ ☐ **Do you ever wonder if the Bible is the true Word of God?** *See page 15.*
- ☐ ☐ **Would you like to know how to trust Jesus more?** *See page 17.*
- ☐ ☐ **Have you ever questioned if God really exists?** *See page 19.*
- ☐ ☐ **Are you wondering what the Trinity is?** *See page 20.*
- ☐ ☐ **Do you need some help dealing with temptations?** *See page 22.*
- ☐ ☐ **Does it bother you when your friends use the Lord's name in vain?** *See page 24.*
- ☐ ☐ **Have you ever wondered how to listen to God?** *See page 25.*
- ☐ ☐ **Do you ever wonder why bad things happen to Christians?** *See page 27.*

1. When I tried to share about God with one of my neighbor friends, she totally shut me out from being a friend. Her parents even got mad. My parents said they wish they could be as strong as I am about witnessing.

It's so hard to share our faith—we feel nervous that other people will think we're weird or snobby because we tell them that Christianity is the only way. And then when people reject us—or get mad at us—it really stings. We think, *Why did this happen? I thought I was doing the right thing!*

The truth is that you did exactly the right thing. And hurray for your parents for encouraging you! Jesus tells us in Mark 16:15, "Go everywhere in the world. Tell the Good News to everyone." That is exactly what you did! Jesus also tells us in Luke 21:17 that people will hate us because we follow Him. Why? Because God shows them the evil things they sometimes choose to do. They want to live their own way, not God's way.

Those words you shared with your friend may end up being very powerful in her life. Did you know that some plant seeds stay inactive and almost unseen for many years before they are ready to sprout and grow? This might be true with your friend, too. Sometime when she is in trouble or lonely or looking for an answer, the words you spoke to her heart may sprout and grow into a search for and a faith in Christ. Keep on obeying and sharing the Good News. God will bless you, and only He knows which seeds will sprout!

Do you know someone who needs to hear the Good News?

When can you tell him or her? How will you do it?
(Through words, sharing a Christian book, etc.)

Go everywhere in the world.
Tell the Good News to everyone!
Mark 16:15

2. How do you know if you are really forgiven or if you are really saved? How do I know I will go to heaven for sure?

Once when I was a girl, I hurt my friend's feelings. When I figured it out, I told her I was sorry and she said she forgave me, but she really didn't. She'd give me rude looks, and she stopped asking me over. She didn't invite me to her birthday party. She didn't mean what she said.

God isn't like that. When He says something, He means it. He tells us that if we ask Him to forgive us, He will. He also tells us that after He forgives us, He completely forgets about it. He never holds a grudge against us, and He doesn't leave us out of His plans or His kingdom because of it. He doesn't remind us about it next time we do something wrong. He is so happy that we can be close with Him, and others, again.

If you have told God that you were truly sorry and asked Him to forgive you because of Jesus Christ, you can be one hundred percent certain that you are forgiven. If you've never done that, you need to go somewhere private and say, "Lord,

I am sorry for all of the wrong things I have done in my life. I know I can't stop sinning without your help. Please forgive me for those sins, because Jesus died for me. Be my friend and in charge of my life from now on. Amen." From then on, you will belong to Him. And whenever you sin again—and you will—you can tell Him you're sorry and ask Him to forgive you again. You'll feel so close to Him afterward it might seem like He's giving you a great big hug!

If you do belong to Christ, you can be certain that you will go to heaven. Jesus tells us that His Father lives in heaven. He promised He was going to prepare a place for us in His Father's house. Enjoy your days on earth, which God has given to you as a gift, and look forward to spending eternity in heaven, a truly awesome place.

Have you ever told God you were sorry for your sins and asked Him to forgive you because Jesus died for you? Is He Lord of your life? How does that show?

What are you most looking forward to about spending time in heaven?

But if we confess our sins, he will forgive our sins. We can trust God. He does what is right. He will make us clean from all the wrongs we have done.

1 John 1:9

3. How do I know that the Bible is the true Word of God?

Whenever we want an answer we can trust, an answer we know is true, one that can guide us as God wants us guided, we can always turn to the Bible. We're told that it is trustworthy for knowing God's will, right? But how do we know that the Bible itself is the true Word of God?

The Scriptures, or papers, that make up the Bible have been copied over thousands of years, from the first person who wrote down the words by hand to the person who is helping to make new translations today using a computer. What do each of these people have in common? They handled something amazingly valuable, something entrusted to them by God. They know God sees if they are careless or dishonest. In Old Testament times, if a scribe (the person copying the Scriptures) made even one mistake, he had to start the entire page all over just to make sure it had no mistakes. Today, many people who love the Lord and have studied His word go over each new translation before it is published. We know what the original writing said for more than ninety-nine percent of the Bible. The Bible does not disagree with itself, and although it can be told from different points of view, we can be sure it is true.

God told people like Jeremiah and Moses to write things down so His people would know what He wanted them to know. Paul tells us he writes under the power given to him by God so he can teach others. First Corinthians 14:37 says that Paul's writings are a "command of the Lord." And most important of all, the Bible itself tells us that Scripture is "God-breathed." Stick out your palm and breathe on it. It came from inside of you. The Scriptures came from inside of God.

There is, of course, a point at which you must trust in faith. Ask yourself: Do you believe that God is powerful enough to create the entire universe just by speaking it into being? Is He able to save all who ask by the sacrifice of His one Son? Does He hold *all* things together, as the Bible says He does? Then isn't He powerful enough to make sure that the words He wanted written down for His people stay pure and whole throughout time? Of course He is.

Is God powerful enough to make sure that the Bible says just what He wants it to say?

Do you believe He watched over the words being written in His book?

All Scripture is given by God.

2 Timothy 3:16a

4. I'd really like to trust in Jesus a little more. How can I do that?

What a terrific goal! When you first meet a new friend in a class or on a sports team or at camp, you don't know very much about each other. You might chat and find out you have a lot in common. After you spend time together—maybe shopping or playing or sleeping over—you trust her more and more. You might tell her some secrets, because now you know she won't blab them. You might ask her for help with something, because now you know she won't laugh at you. You've spent enough time with her to know she can be trusted.

Jesus is many things to us—Lord, Savior, Brother, and Friend. How do we get to know Him better? The same way we get to know our other friends—by hanging out together. You read about Him in the Bible and find out how He treated His friends—and even His enemies. You discover that He is dependable. Talk to other people about Him. Read books about Him. When it's praise and worship time, you close your eyes and spend time worshiping Him. The Bible says God is right there in the middle of our praise, so you're really close to Him when you're praising Him. Then you tell Him your secrets like you would your other friends. You tell Him a funny joke. Sure, He's probably heard it, but He likes to hear from you!

When you've spent some more time together, you'll know Him better. So the next time trouble rolls around (and it always rolls around, doesn't it?) you take a deep breath and say, "Okay, Jesus, I trust you with this." And then you do. You do what you know is right. You talk to people who give you godly answers. You pray. You keep doing those things until the Lord shows you what to do next or shows you that the problem is solved. Trusting someone is like riding a bike—

you can't learn how to do it without actually doing it! The more you ride, the better you get. The more often you trust Jesus, the easier it gets to turn to Him with big and small concerns. Jesus asks us to trust Him, and we know that if He asks us to do something, He will help us to do it and will never let us down.

What problems or concerns do you have right now, this week, in your life?

Will you pray, tell the Lord you trust Him, and ask Him to show you what to do?

Jesus said, "Don't let your hearts be troubled. Trust in God. And trust in me."

John 14:1

5. How do I know God exists? I mean, I can't see Him.

When someone is shocked, she might say, "I can't believe my eyes!" Sometimes it's hard to believe the things right in front of us—like a surprise party or winning a contest we didn't expect to win. Believing in things we can't see is even harder. We live in a world that wants us to "prove it," and proving that God is there isn't easy. God knows this is hard. Believing in Him when we can't see Him with our eyes is part of our faith. Hebrews 11:1 says, "Faith means knowing that something is real even if we don't see it."

How do you know someone is real even when you don't see him or her? One way is to look for other evidence. You've never met me, for example, but you know I exist because you can plainly see my work: this book. When you look around the world and the amazing way it all works, or see your body and the way everything is put together just right, that is proof of God, the Creator. Romans 1:20 says, "There are things about God that people cannot see—his eternal power and all the things that make him God. But since the beginning of the world those things have been easy to understand. They are made clear by what God has made." God lets you know in other ways that He is here. Have you ever prayed about something and then gotten an answer—just sensing the Holy Spirit guiding you, speaking to you through your heart, through your parents, or maybe through a book or a song? The Holy Spirit helps you understand when God is talking to you.

Ask the Lord to open your eyes so that you may see Him, His love, and His work all around you.

When you look at the world around you, what does it teach you about God?

When have you heard the "still, small voice" of God speaking to your heart?

Then Jesus told him, "You believe because you see me. Those who believe without seeing me will be truly happy."

John 20:29

6. I don't understand the Trinity. How can God be Jesus' Father if they and the Holy Spirit are one?

You're a smart girl. This is one of the hardest questions Christians have to deal with, and it's not something that can be completely answered here on earth. Because we don't fully understand it, there is no example that exactly shows how this works, so maybe we can just describe what we do know.

The word *Trinity* isn't in the Bible. It's just the word we use to describe that God is *three* distinct persons but one God. The Father, the Son, and the Holy Spirit all have many different roles—Creator, Savior, and Counselor are three of them, for example—even though they are all One. It's also clear they work together to achieve all that they want to. They are one, but they are also separate. The Father sent the Son to save us. Jesus told us that He was sending the Holy Spirit to help us. The Holy Spirit helps us pray to the Father so we can be close. Each is fully God, and they all work together because, actually, they are one. We are humans, and God is God. He is superior to us, and because He is God we cannot understand everything about Him.

It's exciting to know you will have eternity to ask God these things, isn't it? First Corinthians 13:12 tells us that now we know only things in part, but one day we will know things in full, as fully as God knows us. What a wonderful day that will be!

What questions would you like to ask God when you see Him face-to-face?

Are you looking forward to doing so?

So go and make followers of all people in the world. Baptize them in the name of the Father and the Son and the Holy Spirit.

Matthew 28:19

7. How can I deal with temptations?

Your friends want to sneak into the movie and save the money for candy and popcorn. You really want to look at someone else's paper during a test you didn't have time to study for—you *know* God doesn't want you to get a D. You go to someone's house to sleep over and they all plop down in front of the TV to watch a show you're not allowed to watch. What can you do?

The Bible tells us that God himself never tempts anyone to do something wrong. But people tempt us—for a lot of reasons. Sometimes they don't know it's wrong. Sometimes they do, but they want other people to do it with them so they don't feel bad. Most times, there isn't anyone else tempting us. The temptations are things that come from within ourselves. We can always be sure at those times that the urge to do wrong isn't something that will end up being for our good, no matter how good it seems right now, because it's not in God's plan.

Don't feel guilty when you are tempted. No matter what you're tempted with, you can be sure other people are also tempted with that sin. Being tempted isn't wrong. Everyone, even Jesus, has been tempted. It's giving in to the temptation that's wrong. God, in His goodness, promises to provide a way out of all temptations. Cool!

How does He do that? Well, the Bible says God will not let us be tempted more than we can stand. So we can pray and ask the Lord to help us overcome the temptation. The Bible then says that God will provide a way out. If a group is gossiping, maybe the way out is that someone will call your attention to the other side of the room so you can leave the conversation. If the temptation is to steal something, the Lord might bring to mind the thought that your birthday is coming up and you could ask for it instead. Or you might see the security camera looking down on you. No one can predict the ways the Lord will work—He is creative and kind. Our job is to pray and stand fast when tempted. Keep your eyes and ears open to the way He provides to escape. And then use it!

What are some things you have been tempted to do that you know are not right?

How has the Lord provided a way for you to escape?

The only temptations that you have are the temptations that all people have. But you can trust God. He will not let you be tempted more than you can stand. But when you are tempted, God will also give you a way to escape that temptation.

1 Corinthians 10:13

8. Sometimes when I am around my unsaved friends, they take the Lord's name in vain. I want to say something to them, but I get too shy. What do I do?

It's everywhere, isn't it? On TV, the radio, in conversation. People take the Lord's name in vain, using it as a curse word, when they see something they like, or calling out in surprise. Because your friends probably live in families where people talk that way, they don't see anything wrong. But to people who love the Lord, it can be painful to hear.

Most of the time, your friends won't even know that they're offending you. If they did, they would probably stop, especially if you can be gentle when you tell them. Pray about it and ask the Lord for a humble and gentle spirit, and then talk with your friends in private, one by one, so they don't feel attacked. You could say, "You might not know this, but I'm a Christian. Whenever I hear you say 'God' or 'Jesus Christ,' and I know you're not talking to Him, it hurts my feelings. It's just like if someone said something bad about your mom or dad. Would you mind saying something else when I'm around?"

Most times the person will be embarrassed, and you might be, too. But good friends can overcome that. They will probably try to stop saying these things in front of you, but don't be angry if they slip up or don't realize it from time to time or even if they don't stop at all. They might laugh at you and keep on saying it. The important thing is that you took a stand to honor the Lord's name, even though it was a risky thing for you to do. Jesus says that when we stand up for Him before other people, He stands up for us before His Father.

Do you know anyone who uses the Lord's name in a disrespectful way? Who?

What can you do about it?

If anyone acknowledges me publicly here on earth,
I will openly acknowledge that person
before my Father in heaven.

Matthew 10:32

9. I have a hard time knowing how to listen to God.

The phone rings, and you answer it. "Hello?" you ask. "Hello," the voice says on the other end of the line. "How are you?"

Who's on the other end? If it's your grandma, your best friend, or your mother, you probably recognize the voice right away. If it's someone you don't talk to very often, like an aunt or one of your dad's friends, you might recognize it—

or you might not. If it's a stranger, you won't recognize the voice at all.

This is the way it is with the Lord. When you spend a lot of time with Him, you learn to recognize His voice more often and more easily. It can be a bit tougher to recognize than your friends' voices at first, because you don't hear an out-loud voice. But you definitely can learn to recognize His voice through the ways He *does* speak to us. God always speaks to us through the Bible. When He tells us about a situation with someone in the Bible, He is telling us about ourselves, too. He shows us what happens to someone who doesn't obey—and He is telling us we must obey, too. He shows us Mary Magdalene honoring Jesus with the best she has, and He is telling us, "Give me your best, too, and I will honor you in return." He tells us He loves us through His stories of sacrifice and rescue.

Sometimes God speaks to us through people who give us godly advice or who simply reach out an arm to hug us. God sometimes speaks to us through ideas that pop into our minds after prayer. God can speak to us through songs, books, and the natural world. God speaks to us through our circumstances. Pray and ask the Lord to help you to recognize His voice. You will, because you belong to Him.

When is it easiest for you to hear God's voice?

What can you do to hear His voice more clearly?

After [Jesus] has gathered his own flock, he walks ahead of them, and they follow him because they recognize his voice.

John 10:4 (NLT)

10. Why do bad things happen to Christians sometimes?

Worst-case scenario: You come home one day and your mom sits you down on the couch next to her. She takes your hands in hers and tells you, "I've got cancer." Meanwhile, across the street lives another girl. Her family is not Christian. One day she comes home from school and her mother tells her, "I've got cancer." How will each of you respond?

There are many reasons the Lord allows "bad" things to happen. Sometimes we are being tested. Sometimes it's because we live in a fallen world, and when we try to live purely, we are attacked. The Bible also tells us that God causes rain to fall upon the good people and the bad. He says that both good and bad things happen to those who believe in Him and those who do not. The difference is in how we respond to the things that happen to us. Once we believe in Him, our greatest jobs are to love Him and to be a light so others can find Him, too. One of the ways we do that is by showing our hope and our trust in Him and His faithfulness. If nothing bad ever happened to us, how would we be able to prove our faith to people who don't know Him? They really do watch us when bad things happen. If we still trust, if we have peace that can't be explained, if we hope even while we cry and pray, they will see something they can't find just anywhere. They see that faith is true and strong and that we truly believe we have a Helper who loves and cares for us at all times.

Trust God. He says He can cause all things to work together for good, according to His plan. He didn't spare himself pain—the crucifixion of His son—when it was necessary, did He? Next time something bad happens to you or to someone you love, ask yourself, "How can I let my light shine before others in this situation?" It doesn't mean you won't be sad or angry or concerned. Of course you will! But you can also show anyone watching—and prove to yourself—that God is faithful in good times and bad. Sometimes the answer to prayer takes longer than you'd like. Sometimes it never comes out as you wish it would. No matter what, God will help it to be all right in the end, and you'll build up the faith of those who are watching you.

When is it hard for you to trust God?

Who in your life is watching you, seeing what your faith really means when it is tested?

You will be my witnesses—in Jerusalem, in all of Judea, in Samaria, and in every part of the world.

Acts 1:8b

Family

God sets the lonely in families.

Psalm 68:6 (NIV)

Quiz

YES	NO	
☐	☐	**Do you worry when your parents yell?** *See page 32.*
☐	☐	**Is controlling your anger a problem?** *See page 33.*
☐	☐	**Do you wonder why other kids can do things that your parents won't let you do?** *See page 35.*
☐	☐	**Does your family embarrass you?** *See page 36.*
☐	☐	**Are you ever mad that your parents let your brothers or sisters do things they won't let you do?** *See page 38.*
☐	☐	**Do you need some good ideas on how to talk to your parents without being embarrassed?** *See page 40.*
☐	☐	**Do you need to know what you can do instead of talking back to your parents?** *See page 41.*
☐	☐	**Have you wondered what you can do to heal the hurt of your parents' divorce?** *See page 43.*
☐	☐	**Is there someone in your family you fight with a lot?** *See page 45.*
☐	☐	**Do you feel you are disciplined more often than your brothers and sisters?** *See page 46.*

1. My parents yell at each other and sometimes at me. I really hate it when they yell. I worry about them getting a divorce. Then I want to yell back.

It can make you so nervous to listen to your parents yell. After all, your whole world seems to rest on what they do, what they decide, how they act. They're your sense of safety! And when that's in danger, it feels scary. When they yell at us, it can also make us feel small.

Really, though, your parents are probably just tired and stressed. It's hard to be an adult. When you're a kid, you think it will be so cool to be an adult—you get to do your own thing and make your own rules. But when you *are* an adult, it's hard to have so many responsibilities. One of the most important responsibilities your parents have is taking care of you. They're probably trying hard. Stress overwhelms us, and when overwhelmed, even the best parents might yell. It doesn't mean they don't love you, and it doesn't mean they don't love each other or that they're going to get a divorce.

You can't control your parents, but you can control yourself by not yelling back. Some of the most important jobs a kid has are to love, honor, and obey her parents. The Bible says that if we honor our parents, it will go well with us. It's God's promise!

Your parents' yelling upsets you, so respectfully talk with your parents during a calm, relaxed time. Tell them how you feel. Tell them when you notice it most, that it worries you, and how you feel when you're yelled at. Most likely it will change how they act, because parents work hard to make their kids feel safe and loved. But even if it doesn't, keep doing what you know is right. Honor your parents in how *you* talk to them—and to others. No matter what someone else does, you can always choose what is right.

Do your parents ever talk to each other in a way that worries you?

What are two things you can do?

The command says, "Honor your father and mother." This is the first command that has a promise with it. The promise is: "Then everything will be well with you, and you will have a long life on the earth."

Ephesians 6:2

2. Sometimes I have trouble because I do mean things, like hit my little sister because she is bugging me. How can I change?

It's terrific to have brothers and sisters, but sometimes it can be hard, too. I have a little brother and a little sister, and lots of times I felt I had to bc in charge of them when I didn't want to be. It made me angry, and when we're angry it's easy to lose self-control. In the end, I had to decide what kind of a person I wanted to be. I had to make up my mind that I was going to do the right thing. You have to do that, too. And you can!

You've got a great start deciding that you don't like how you react. Now think about what you're going to do instead of being mean or hitting. Could you go somewhere alone and cool off? Later come back and talk about what made you mad. Maybe it won't seem so important in a few minutes. If you feel like hitting your sister, stuff your hands into your pockets or put them down at your sides—or come up with your own ideas. The important thing is to have a habit of doing something right while you wait for your anger to cool down. It's hard to think straight when you're mad.

The Bible tells us that we have many blessings. Because of those blessings, God wants us to keep adding good things to our lives. You've already said you want to change. Why not start with self-control and kindness toward your brothers and sisters? They'll feel better, and so will you. Later, read the rest of the 2 Peter verses for more wonderful things to add to your life. Pray and ask God to help you with this. He will. Depend on it!

What can you do to add these things to your life?

Self-control:

Kindness to your brothers and sisters:

Because you have these blessings, you should try as much as you can to add these things to your lives... to your knowledge, add self-control... to your service for God, add kindness for your brothers and sisters in Christ.

1 Peter 1:5–7

3. Why won't my parents allow me to do what other girls are allowed to do, even if the other girls and their families are Christians?

Ever notice how your parents know things about you that no one else does—like how your mom never puts gobs of peanut butter on your sandwich since you like only a little bit? Or that your dad never teases you in front of other people because he knows it embarrasses you? Lots of things are special about you, and lots of things are unique to your family. Every family is one of a kind.

When God set you in a family, He in His wisdom chose your parents, chose the brothers and sisters you would have, and formed your personality and how you would look. He gave you parents who would understand you. He also gave your parents an awesome—and fearsome—responsibility: to raise you in the way He requires. Your parents are responsible to God for that. When they meet Him face-to-face, they will have to answer to Him for the choices they made for you.

God has given your parents wisdom in raising you and your one-of-a-kind family. If you'd like them to think again about a decision on a movie or a TV show or clothing, you certainly can ask them to do so. But if they say no again, don't pester them or grow bitter. Be thankful that you have parents who truly understand you, even when you are *sure* that they don't. They seek to do the best for you. The Bible says their teaching is like a light and helps you to have life.

What rules do you have that are hard to follow?

How do you think your parents might be trying to protect you with these rules?
(Hint: If you don't know, ask!)

My [child], keep your father's commands. Don't forget your mother's teaching. . . . Their commands are like a lamp. Their teaching is like a light. And the correction that comes from them helps you have life.

Proverbs 6:20, 23

4. I feel like my family is weird and everyone else's family is normal. Why can't I stop comparing my family to everyone else's?

Most of the time I feel just fine about my clothes or my stuff—until I go to the mall or read the ads in the Sunday paper. Suddenly my clothes look a little out of touch. And my gear looks a bit, um . . . ragged. What was fine before isn't fine anymore. Why not? Because I begin to compare.

To compare means to measure one thing against something else. When we measure, one ends up being better, bigger, and cooler than the other. They almost never come out equal. That's how it is when you begin to compare your family with other families. Because you know annoying little things about your family, like your dad sneezing in a totally embarrassing way or your mom tweezing her eyebrows while she's driving, your family might start to look weird compared to other families. Other people's sisters seem nicer, their brothers seem cuter. But guess what? They're probably thinking the same thing about your family!

The secret to being happy is contentment, or being satisfied with what you have. It doesn't mean that you can't ever buy a new outfit or paint your room that cool frosty lavender you've wanted to try. But it does mean that you choose to be happy with what you have, not always comparing what you have with what someone else has, whether it's their clothes or their family. The Bible says that God sets people in families, meaning He chooses for them. Be content with what God, in His great love, has chosen for you.

What fun things does your family do together?

What are you thankful about in your family?

God sets the lonely in families.

Psalm 68:6 (NIV)

5. My sister is older than I am, and she gets to do *everything*! Now my mom won't let me do things she let my sister do when she was my age. How can I tell my mom that I grew up?

When we're five we can get a library card. When we're sixteen we can learn to drive. We start to expect that everything should happen to us at a certain age. But really, most things happen because of a combination of how old we are *and* how responsible we are. This is also true (though it doesn't feel good to hear it): Some things aren't safe for kids, and parents protect their children by forbidding them to do those things.

Maybe your parents let your sister do something at an early age and it didn't work out well, so they're making a better plan for you. Maybe they're not aware of something you want to do, something you feel you deserve to do. Maybe you've been irresponsible in some way, and they're not ready to trust you with other things. Those are hard things to think about, but you have to look at them honestly before you can solve your problem.

The Bible tells us that when we are trusted with something small, we have to prove ourselves with that before we should be given more. If there's something special you want to be allowed to do, ask your mom. Explain that you are willing to prove you're trustworthy. If it's something she feels isn't right for you, respect and live with that decision. If it's a matter of your being faithful and trustworthy, ask how you can prove that. She may ask you to stop sassing or to do your schoolwork without being asked or to clean your room. All of these things help her understand that you're a more grown-up girl. Keep on this path of being faithful with the little things. You'll be surprised at the big things people will trust you with once you've proven yourself!

How do you respond when your parents tell you "no"?

Ask your mom how you could be more trustworthy. What did she say?

A person who is trusted with something must show that he is worthy of that trust.

1 Corinthians 4:2

6. Why can't I talk to my parents without being embarrassed?

When we're little, we have easy things to talk about with our parents—can we play with a certain toy, may we please be excused from the table, will you read me a book? As we grow older, our concerns are different. A lot of the things we want to discuss with our parents can be embarrassing or hard. On top of it all, we're not sure how our parents will answer. Do they still think we're little girls, or do they realize we are growing up?

Many girls have questions about their bodies, about their feelings, about scary things they think about but never tell anyone else. Trust me, all of those topics are normal even though you don't hear anyone else talk about them. Perhaps you tried to talk with your parents about these at one time, and they were rushed or for some other reason didn't recognize how important it was. If they gave you a quick answer or a brush-off, you may feel afraid to bring the subject up again. Maybe you just think that the stuff you want to say is weird.

Be brave and speak up! God gave you parents to love you and guide you. He gives them wisdom to do it. Chances are, the topics won't be as embarrassing to them as they are to you. After all, they had questions when they were kids. If you feel more comfortable talking with one parent than the other, wait till you have some time alone. Ask for it. Pray and ask the Lord for the right words, then dive right in. The hardest part will be opening your mouth and getting the first sentence out. Many people in the Bible had a hard time getting started saying what needed to be said because they were afraid. The Lord will help you, and I know you have the guts to do it. Remember, the only silly question is the one that goes unasked.

What questions do you have that you've been too embarrassed to ask your parents?

When will you be brave and ask?

Now go! I will help you speak. I will tell you what to say.

Exodus 4:12

7. I need some good Bible verses to think of when I want to talk back to my parents or say something I shouldn't to my brothers.

The book of James says that our entire body is like a ship. The rudder is a very small part, but it steers the ship. The man who controls the rudder controls the ship. If our body is the ship, our rudder is our tiny, teeny, major-powerful tongue. Our tongue can drive our ship into the sharp rocks and hurt ourselves and those around us if we're not careful. One game we played in my family was to squeeze all of the toothpaste out of the tube and then offer ten dollars to anyone who could put it all back in with a spoon. It couldn't be done. It's the same way with your words—once they're out of your mouth, they can't be taken back. No matter what.

You are a *smart* girl to figure out that you need some tools to help you control your tongue. You're even smarter to know where to go to get help. When we memorize the Word of God, the Holy Spirit can bring it to our minds at just the right time to stop our tongues before they stop us!

Here are some good verses to choose from:

> Whoever is careful about what he says protects his life. But anyone who speaks without thinking will be ruined. Proverbs 13:3

> A gentle answer will calm a person's anger. But an unkind answer will cause more anger. Proverbs 15:1

> A wise person is known for his understanding. He wins people to his side with pleasant words. Proverbs 16:21

Which of these verses will you memorize to help you control your words?

Check off this box when you've copied your verse and hung it up in your room. ☐

Whoever is careful about what he says protects his life.

Proverbs 3:13a

8. My parents are getting a divorce. How do I heal the hurt? And how can I keep in touch with both families?

A parent's divorce is one of the hardest things a kid may ever have to deal with. So the first thing is, a divorce is in *no* way your fault. Never. And it is very hard to deal with, but you don't have to go through it alone. Sit in a quiet place and pour your heart out to God. Tell Him how sad you are about the whole situation, that you feel hurt and angry, and whatever else your true feelings are. God is not uncomfortable hearing your strong feelings. He wants you to be honest with Him. Pray and ask the Lord to help you make it through the hard days. Just when you think you've got it all taken care of, something else will come up and you'll feel hurt all over again.

The great news is that you *can* handle it with God's help. God has many names; some of them will help you remember what He will do for you in this (and any other) tough situation. He is called Comforter and Counselor. His comfort and counsel will help to heal your hurt. He is a Friend. He is a strong Rock who will never leave you. He is a mighty Help in time of trouble. People will let us down because they are human. God will never let you down.

You need to talk with your mom and dad about your fear that once they are divorced you won't be able to keep in touch with each family. Ask them to set up times to make sure you get to see all of your grandparents and cousins, if that's what worries you. Brainstorm some special things you do with each of them—hiking only with Dad, for example, or maybe the two of you have dinner together the first Thursday of every month. Maybe you and your mom can do your clothes shopping, or the two of you can have a beauty night one Saturday each month. If you set up special routines with each person you want to stay close to, it will help you set aside time for each other.

Do you worry about not being able to spend time with someone in your family (even if they're not divorced)?

What routines can you set up so you can spend more time together?

The Lord defends those who suffer. He protects them in times of trouble. Those who know the Lord trust Him. He will not leave those who come to Him.

Psalm 9:9–10

9. My cousin and I are like enemies. We argue all the time and usually have one really big fight every year. We are Christians, even though we forget it when we are around each other. It was humiliating today because in Sunday school we talked about loving your neighbor. How will we ever get along?

When I was a girl, one of my distant cousins and I were really good friends. Then we got cool toward each other. Pretty soon we didn't talk at all. Guess why? Jealousy—and each of us thinking we were better than the other. Not a very pretty picture, was it? Plus, we could have had a lot of fun together if we had just changed our attitudes. Instead, we missed out on a lot of good times.

You have asked a wise question. You already know something is wrong, and you know that the way you act toward each other isn't very Christlike. The Bible says people will know we are Christians by the way we love one another. Loving is a very important part of being a Christian, maybe the most important after following Christ. So here's a little prescription for peace with your cousin. You can't make her follow it, but you can. I'll bet if you change the way you act, she'll change the way she acts, too. Love is hard to resist.

1. Tell her you are sorry if you've done anything to hurt her feelings.
2. Ask her if there is anything you can do to make your friendship smoother.
3. Be kind to her, putting her interests above your own.

This will not be easy. In fact, it will be hard. You've been fighting a long time, and our pride does not want us to put others before ourselves. If we call ourselves Christians, we must choose to act as Christ did. Unselfishly. You can do it, girl.

Is there someone you fight with a lot?

What can you do to put that person's needs above your own?

When you do things, do not let selfishness or pride be your guide. Be humble and give more honor to others than to yourselves. Do not be interested only in your own life, but be interested in the lives of others. In your lives you must think and act like Christ Jesus.

Philippians 2:3–5

10. My parents discipline me *way* more than they discipline my brother. And when there's a problem, I always get in trouble first. I think it's unfair, but what can I do?

It hurts when you feel someone's picking on you, doesn't it? And sometimes when our hearts ache, we allow a hard little knot to grow inside them, thinking that will stop us from being hurt again. This is just what the Evil One wants us to do in a situation like yours.

But maybe things aren't exactly what they seem to be. Perhaps your mom and dad know you're a responsible young lady and expect more from you. Maybe you're older so your name comes out first. It might be that your parents call on your brother as much as you, but it doesn't seem that way when it's you in the hot seat! Maybe you *are* disobeying more. Or perhaps they're just tired and trying to solve the problem quickly.

No matter what the cause, the Bible tells us if we are angry, we're to work things out as soon as possible. This is really hard, because the *last* person you feel like talking to is the person who hurt your feelings. Wait until everyone's tempers cool down—maybe an hour or two. Then ask your mom and/or dad if you could talk with them alone. Explain that when they shout at you or always call you first when there's a problem, it makes you feel less loved or like you're always to blame. Then listen to their perspective on the situation, too. Ask if there's something you can do together to solve the problem. Then hug one another tightly and feel that heart knot melt away.

Are you angry with anyone?

What should you do? When will you do it?

And "don't sin by letting anger gain control over you." Don't let the sun go down while you are still angry, for anger gives a mighty foothold to the Devil.

Ephesians 4:26–27 (NLT)

Friendship

Two people are better than one. They get more done by working together. If one person falls, the other can help him up.

Ecclesiastes 4:9–10a

Quiz

YES	NO	
☐	☐	**Do you have friends who are too bossy?** *See page 52.*
☐	☐	**Is anyone pestering you to be friends?** *See page 53.*
☐	☐	**Do you feel like people won't accept you the way you are?** *See page 55.*
☐	☐	**Would you confront a friend who is boy crazy?** *See page 56.*
☐	☐	**Have you ever wondered if a friend was really a Christian?** *See page 58.*
☐	☐	**Do you have a friend who wants you to do something you know is wrong?** *See page 60.*
☐	☐	**Are you worried about losing your friends?** *See page 62.*
☐	☐	**Do you know what to do about gossip?** *See page 63.*
☐	☐	**Do you want to be in the popular group?** *See page 65.*
☐	☐	**Are you ever jealous when a friend is with other people?** *See page 67.*

1. I have this friend, or so I think. Some days she likes me, but she's always bossing me around or leaving me. When we get into a fight, I'm always the one apologizing first. What should I do?

Friendships provide us with some of our *best* times. Sometimes, though, we give our hearts to friends who don't treat us kindly. That can mean some of our *worst* times! I remember the day I ran up to Kim, who I thought was my best friend. She was talking with another girl, and when I stood next to her, she shouted, "Just leave me alone!" I practically burst out in tears and promised myself I'd never talk to her again. After a few days apart, Kim asked me if I wanted to come over. I had some decisions to make. And so do you.

One choice you could make would be to do whatever she tells you to do. That would work for a while, but she'd get sick of your following her around. And you are already sick of her bossing you. Another choice is to stop being friends. It sounds like you do enjoy her company sometimes, so both of you might miss out on some good times if you did that.

Friendships are about loving one another. The Bible says that love is patient and kind. Speak with your friend. Perhaps she feels that you aren't giving her enough breathing space or enough room to be friends with other girls, too. Maybe that's why she leaves you. Be patient with her; allow her to be friends with you and also with others. Next time she bosses you, tell her how hurt you feel. She might not realize how bossy she is and would treat you more kindly once it's pointed out to her.

If the two of you can't work out being patient and kind with each other, maybe you need to reconsider your friendship. When someone continues to be mean after you've talked about it, it might be time for a new friend.

Do you have a friend who treats you unkindly? What can you do?

Is there a friend whom you treat unkindly? How can you change?

Love is patient and kind.

1 Corinthians 13:4a

2. This one girl always follows me and my friend around at school and copies us. She even made sure her locker was next to ours. She is completely spoiled. We hate her so much.

Words can be powerful weapons. Remember the saying, "Sticks and stones may break my bones, but words will never hurt me"? Well, that's a lie. The hurts caused by words are stronger and last longer than almost any hurt to your bones. When you say you hate someone, it's like kicking her in the heart.

But your feelings matter, too. Your feelings of hate come from your anger at not being left alone and from your helplessness to stop her from trailing after you. You don't feel like you have any control. It's understandable that you'd want some time to yourself and with your friend. If you can get some control over this situation, you'll feel less angry and less likely to say or do something you'll regret later.

So . . . does this mean you have to be best friends with the girl who follows you? No. Does it mean you have to be friends with her at all? No. Does it mean that you have to treat her gently and with respect? Yes. If you have a problem with someone, talk with her. Chances are, she feels really insecure and doesn't have many friends of her own. That's why she's following you around. She's copying you because she admires you. If you are kind to her, it will show Jesus' kind of love. Now, *that* would be something for people to copy! If you are unkind, it will only harden your own heart and change you from the person you are into a person you don't want to be. Being mean can destroy you.

Quietly ask her to please stop following you around. If she keeps doing it, ask a teacher or parent for help.

How can you deal with a friendship issue?

Who can help you with this?

Your own soul is nourished when you are kind, but you destroy yourself when you are cruel.

Proverbs 11:17 (NLT)

3. What do I do if my friends try to act cool and I don't get it, and then they make fun of me and won't stop teasing me?

Cool is really hard to keep up with. Words and songs and clothes that are cool one day are out of it the next week. You can spend a lot of time trying to be cool. Some of it might make you feel good. Some of it will make you feel like you're running in a race that you will never, ever win. It's important to fit in, to belong with a group of others, no doubt about it. The real question is: fit in and belong with whom?

A real friend doesn't care if you're cool according to what other kids think. She thinks you're cool because she knows all about you and thinks you're terrific. A real friend sticks up for you even when it's hard. One time when I was a kid, a group of girls tried to corner me after school. They didn't think I was cool, and they thought they were. My friend Cathy ran past them to get into the school to get help. They tried to stop her, and she pushed past them. They told her they'd hate her if she helped me. She didn't care. She got help and stood by me. She liked me for the person I was inside, not because I could make her seem cooler by being her friend. In fact, at that moment, being my friend made her less cool. A girl is not a true friend if she only likes you if you make her more popular.

Why do you want to be friends with these girls? Do you

feel cooler when you're with them? I'm sure you don't enjoy being made fun of and teased and don't want to do that with others. It may seem like you'll have more power if you're their friend, but they are showing you the nasty ways they're using that power. A real friend will stick by you no matter what trouble comes your way. She doesn't care if other people think you're cool or if they think you're not. If you fit in and belong with girls like that, you'll find that having power won't matter at all.

Why do you sometimes want others to think you're cool?

Are you willing to hang out with kids who make you uncomfortable in order to be cool? Who?

A friend loves at all times.

Proverbs 17:17a (NIV)

4. My friend is totally boy crazy. Every week it seems she

has a new boyfriend. How can I show her that there is much more to life than boys, boys, boys?

When I was twelve, my friend Kristen had a crush on a boy named Mike. Pretty soon, she was passing notes to him, trying to get us to sit by him, talking about him all the time—even if I tried to change the subject. She always wanted to call him on the phone. Finally, when she kept writing Mike's name all over the bottom of her sneakers, I said something to her.

It's not that I thought being interested in boys was totally wrong. In fact, there were some boys that I thought were interesting, too. We talked about them and even to them sometimes. It's just that they didn't take over my life. I thought about other things, talked about other things, and had a good time without them.

Tell your friend how you feel. Tell her that every now and then it's interesting to talk about boys and that you don't mind doing that sometimes. But you miss talking about the other things you used to discuss, too. You miss giggling about clothes and talking about what job you want to have when you grow up or where you want to live. You miss her company! If you feel that she's boy crazy, other people probably do, too. But they might not be brave enough to say something. A good friend will tell you if you're doing something wrong or something that pushes others away. It doesn't feel good to be confronted (and it might be uncomfortable to confront her), so she might feel hurt at first. A true friend will do that, though, because she knows it's the best thing for her friend. And just think of the reward—your old best buddy back!

Do you have a friend who is doing something that

makes you uncomfortable?

What can you say to her about it in a kind, loving way?

Wounds from a friend are better than many kisses from an enemy.

Proverbs 27:6

5. I'm beginning to wonder if my friend is a Christian!

When we grow up in a family that loves Christ, it is easy for us to think that everyone who is nice is a Christian, too. Many people think they are Christians when they may not be. When I was a girl, I thought I was a Christian because my family went to church on Christmas and Easter and because we weren't Jewish or Buddhist or anything else. I was a nice girl. If someone had asked me if I was a Christian, I would have said yes. But I wasn't a Christian.

Why not? A person isn't a Christian just because she goes to church, because she's not another religion, or even because she calls herself one. A person is a Christian because she has trusted Jesus Christ for salvation. It's a two-way matter. When someone holds out a gift to you, it's not yours until you decide to reach out and take it. In the same way, Jesus offers himself as Savior, but you are not a Christian until you decide to reach out and accept the offer. That is what calling on His name means. I didn't call upon His name and accept His offer of salvation till I was nineteen. I didn't understand that I needed to. Your friend might not understand that, either.

When you are a Christian, the Holy Spirit helps you tell the difference between someone who has faith and someone who does not. Maybe you're sensing that your friend believes she's a Christian but isn't. Perhaps no one has told her Jesus has made the offer, but she herself has to reach out and make a decision to accept it. Most exciting of all, maybe God has put you together as friends so *you* can help her understand!

Why not wait till a private moment together and tell her, "There's something I didn't always understand, and maybe you don't, either. Did you know you have to ask Jesus to be your Lord and Savior before you can be a Christian?" You could tell her how you prayed and told Jesus you were sorry for your sins, how you wanted Him to help you and be your Savior forever. Ask her if she feels the same way. If she does, you can pray it together. If she's already done that, you can feel sure your friend is a Christian and you've done a good thing by checking.

Which of your friends might think they are Christians but maybe don't understand what that means?

Will you pray for and talk with them about it?

And everyone who calls on the name of the Lord will be saved.

Acts 2:21

6. My friend's brother started smoking, and now my friend is smoking, too. I know she's going to try to get me to do it, too, and if I say no, she probably won't want to be my friend anymore. We've been friends since first grade, and I don't want our friendship to end.

It's very hard to sit by and watch your friend go down a wrong path, especially someone you've been friends with for a long time. You sound a little fearful, too, that you're going to have to choose—between keeping your friend while doing something you know is wrong (smoking) and losing your friend when you refuse to smoke. I think you might need to make that choice now, even if she doesn't ask you to smoke. Why?

Have you heard the saying, "One bad apple spoils the whole barrel"? When you pick apples, you look them over very carefully to make sure they don't have any bruises on them. Bruises are the soft spots that taste bad, and if there's even a teeny tiny bruise on the apple the day you pick it, within a few days the entire apple will be bad. If that's not bad enough, the bruises spread from one apple to another. The whole barrel of healthy apples will go bad within a short time just by being near a bruised apple.

Your friend has taken on a very unhealthy habit. She gave in to pressure from her brother to smoke. Who knows what kind of pressure she might give in to next? And you already feel that you might have to make a trade-off with her to keep her friendship. You don't want to do something you know to be wrong. The Bible tells us that to honor the Lord we must obey the law of the land. The law of this land says it's illegal for kids to smoke.

In order to protect you, the Bible also tells us that we are to stay away from people who are doing wrong things. It doesn't tell us to stay away from them only when they're doing wrong; it just says to stay away from them. Why? Because everyone is able to be tempted. Sooner or later your good habits will be set aside, and like the apple, you'll end up bruised. Although you may need to tell your friend she'll have to choose between smoking and you, you don't have to give up on her. Faithfully praying for her is a way to express your love and concern even when you can't be together.

Do you know someone who is doing something wrong?

What should you do?

Do not be fooled: "Bad friends will ruin good habits."

1 Corinthians 15:33

7. I am worried that I will lose my friends when my mom starts homeschooling me next year. Any advice?

Your whole life is changing, isn't it? New way of learning, more time with your mom and dad, more time with brothers and sisters, no teachers . . . And now you think, no friends. But it might not be what it seems. How do you normally make friends? Your friends are probably people you live by, people you went to school with or played on teams with. Perhaps your friends are people you know at church. When you first met them, it was because you had something in common. The things that *kept* you friends were doing things together you both liked and spending time together.

This will be true with your new homeschool adventure. You can still keep the old friends. Ask your mom to help arrange times when you and your friends can get together, maybe for a sleepover or to go shopping. But also remember that you will have a whole new group of people in your life. There will be other kids you come to know who are homeschooled. Guess what? It'll be like when you first made friends at school—you'll have something in common and you'll do things together that build your friendship.

God knows we need friends. Trust Him to help provide you with friends throughout your life. Keep your eyes open to all the kids around you, and keep your mind open to saying, "Hello, what's your name?" to someone new. Remember, to make a friend, you need to be a friend first. Keep an open heart toward the people you meet. Sometimes the person we think we could never be friends with turns out to be the very person God placed in our path to be a best pal.

What are you worried about with friends?

Does Jesus know what you need? Can you trust Him to provide for your needs?

Your Father knows the things you need before you ask him.

Matthew 6:8b

8. Gossip is a big problem. What should you do when someone is gossiping about someone else right in front of you? Or what if you find out someone is gossiping about you?

There is almost nothing worse than finding out that someone has backstabbed you—told your secrets or made up lies about you. The only thing worse is when someone spreads them around. I'll never forget the day I walked out onto the field to say hi to all of my friends on a softball team. Some of them looked away from me, and some of them said hi and then walked away. Three stood in a corner, looking at me from behind their caps and talking in low voices. One of them wouldn't look me in the eye. She'd started the gossip.

Proverbs 11:13 tells us that a person who gossips can't keep secrets, but a trustworthy person can keep a secret. If someone shared a secret with you, she has trusted you with a little part of herself. If you break that trust and tell someone else, you are proving that you can't be trusted, that gossiping is more important than a friend.

Proverbs 26:20 says that a fire without wood will go out, and without gossip, quarreling will stop. Once people stop talking about an issue, people lose interest and forget about it. Once they forget about it, it's not causing trouble anymore.

What should you do when someone is gossiping in front of you? Think of how awful it is when someone blurts your secrets to a crowd. You hate it! So protect the person who is being gossiped about. Be brave—speak up and say it's not a nice thing to talk about. Change the subject. Stopping the gossip in that way will be like pouring water on the fire. If someone gossips all the time, that person is not to be trusted. Is that really the kind of friend you want? You might think again about hanging out with people who enjoy gossip.

What should you do when someone gossips about you? If you hear about it, you might privately tell that person it hurt your feelings when you heard about it. Then say nothing more and let the fire die out.

Do you know anyone who has a problem with gossip? Who?

What can you do to help stop gossip?

An evil person causes trouble, and a person who gossips ruins friendships.

Proverbs 16:28

9. I don't mean to brag, but I'm pretty popular this year. I have a hard enough time doing stuff with all of my new friends, but now my old friend from last year, who isn't popular, still wants to be friends. How can I tell her that we're not friends anymore?

It sounds as if you think you're moving up the social ladder—you have places to go, and you don't want anyone to hold you back. It's nice that you are popular and enjoying your new friends. But are you the kind of girl who leaves friends in the dust?

The Bible is clear that Jesus was not popular. Some people picked on Him. Some people made fun of Him. He had no great big house for people to admire—in fact, He didn't have a house at all. His friends were, for the most part, not the rich and famous and powerful. They were the people that other people left in the dust.

If we are Christians, we should become a little more like Jesus every day. The Bible says that God does not look at the outward appearance of a person: what kind of clothes she wears, if she's pretty, if she has a lot of cool things. God looks at what is inside a person—for example, if she is more interested in people or power, or if she is giving or selfish. If you are a Christian, ask yourself, "Am I becoming a little more like Jesus each day?"

Have you heard the song that begins, "Make new friends, but keep the old; one is silver and the other gold"? Your new friends are fine—enjoy them! But they're silver. The friends who stay with you a long time and love you for yourself are gold. Cherish them, too.

Whom have you left in the dust because they aren't popular enough?

How could you become a little more like Jesus every day?

Do not be proud, but make friends with those who seem unimportant. Do not think how smart you are.

Romans 12:16b

10. My best friend has been hanging out with someone else—she even slept over at her house. I think it's rude, and I want to tell that other girl to back off and not steal my best friend. Should I say it?

Whenever you have a best friend, it's like you've given her a little piece of yourself. You share secrets and giggle and count on her in times of trouble. If that friend pulls away, it's scary! You might think, *Who will be my special friend now?*

You know what? It's healthy—and fun—to have more than one friend! Sometimes being with only one friend is like eating only one kind of fruit. Apples may be tasty, but bananas are, too. Or like reading only one kind of book when there are lots of great stories out there. Your friend might want to see what other friends have to share, and you could, too.

Don't say anything mean about your friend's new pal—and try not to think anything mean, either. It won't help your friendship, and it will only hurt people—including you. Instead, tell your best friend, "I've missed being together. Do you want to come over this weekend?" And *you* make some new friends, too! Think about a girl you'd like to know better. Be brave! Ask her, "Want to be my partner on this assignment?" or say, "Sit here!" at Sunday school and pat the seat beside you. Then you'll have several special friends to share things with.

What could you say and do if your best bud wants some other friends, too?

Name at least one person you would like to be better friends with.

May the words of my mouth and the thoughts of my heart be pleasing to you, O Lord, my rock and my redeemer.

Psalm 19:14 (NLT)

School

Teach the wise, and they will be wiser. Teach the righteous, and they will learn more.

Proverbs 9:9

Quiz

YES	NO	
☐	☐	**Do you ever wonder why they don't just put God back in the schools?** *See page 72.*
☐	☐	**Does anyone ever copy your work?** *See page 73.*
☐	☐	**Has a mean teacher ever annoyed you?** *See page 75.*
☐	☐	**Do you have a problem talking too much in class?** *See page 77.*
☐	☐	**Do you ever feel behind in some subjects?** *See page 78.*
☐	☐	**Would you like to try a different kind of schooling?** *See page 80.*
☐	☐	**Does it bother you when you don't get the grades you deserve?** *See page 82.*
☐	☐	**Has anyone ever picked on you because you know a lot?** *See page 84.*
☐	☐	**Are you worried there will be a shooting at your school?** *See page 85.*
☐	☐	**Does it trouble you that your grades aren't good enough?** *See page 87.*

1. Why don't people have a vote and put God in schools again?

When the United States of America was made a nation, the Founding Fathers wrote our Constitution. The Constitution was one of the papers that everyone agreed would help to govern the country. That's why we call it government. It is how we govern, or manage, all the people, places, and things in the U.S. It helps us make decisions about what we as a nation do and don't do.

One of the things the Constitution said was that the government can't dictate an official religion. This is called separation of church and state, or separation between the government and any religion. Before the Constitution was written, in most countries the king decided for his citizens what faith they would have, and they had no choice in it. Our Founding Fathers wanted everyone to be able to choose their own faith. After all, Christianity is about someone choosing to follow Jesus; no one is a Christian just because of where she was born.

Some people took that separation to mean there could be no mention of God in any place that had to do with the government. Most Christians, however, believe that was not what the Founding Fathers had in mind—we still have *In God We Trust* on our coins, for example. Many of the Founding Fathers were strong Christians. But today the courts have decided that the Constitution meant no mention of God in places that receive money from the government, and that means public schools, too.

God has His people everywhere, even in the courts and schools. The Bible says that God can turn the thoughts of kings like rivers of water. He can also turn the thoughts of judges and presidents and everyone else who makes decisions. The Bible tells us to obey the laws of our land, but we can pray that our leaders will open their ears to the Lord. Even if people don't recognize God, leave Him out of their decisions, or pretend He doesn't exist, God is still in charge. No matter who is in charge of the government or the schools, take comfort in the fact that God is always in control.

How often do you pray for the people who are in our government?

What is the name of one person in government you could pray for right now?

God is King over the nations. . . . Even the leaders of the earth belong to God. He is supreme.

Psalm 47:8–9

2. One girl copies my work all the time, and it really annoys me.

Of course it annoys you—and it should! You've worked hard to study, and someone who didn't is trying to take advantage of your hard work. She's not helping herself by copying you—she can't copy you for the rest of her life. She will have to know how to spell, write, and do math. It's not fair to you, either.

The hard thing—but the thing you're going to have to do—is to speak up. That girl is doing something wrong, and you caught her. Until someone corrects her, she's going to keep doing it. You might take her aside and gently say, "Please don't copy off of my paper anymore. It's not fair to either of us." If she tries to look on your paper, cover it up with your hand and look her straight in the eye so she knows that *you* know what she's trying to do. If she keeps copying your work or someone else's, it would be wise to tell your teacher in private. Teachers are there to help you learn, and the teacher can't help this girl learn if she doesn't know she's not answering the questions on her own.

The Bible tells us to speak up when we have problems. It can be one of the hardest things in the world. It's much easier to keep quiet and not have trouble. But the real trouble comes when we don't tackle a problem. Since you know she's cheating, you need to be part of the solution whether you want to or not! Don't worry, though. The Lord will give you strength to say what needs to be said. He can work this situation out to be good for both of you.

Is anyone cheating off of you? Who?

When can you talk to them? What will you do?

Someone in your group might do something wrong. You who are spiritual should go to him and help make him right again. You should do this in a gentle way.

Galatians 6:1a

3. My friends and I have a very hard time with our music teacher. She is always yelling and punishing us unfairly. When anyone else is watching her, she is very sweet and nice so no other teachers know. What can we do?

Each snowflake God created is made of the same material—snow. Each has a similar shape to other snowflakes. They all melt. But they are all different, no two alike. People are the same way. God made all of us, and we look alike. But we are all different, too. Because of this, we don't always automatically get along with everyone—because other people see things differently than we do. We each have different backgrounds and different goals and different ways of dealing with things. Your teacher might handle problems differently than you do.

Just for a minute, try to see things from the teacher's perspective. She might have other classes that are really disobedient. She could be stressed from that and overreact to your class. It's not fair, but it happens. Maybe she *is* just acting sweet in front of others, or maybe she's sweet to other adults because she's more comfortable with them. Maybe someone in your group laughed, and she thought you were laughing at her. Maybe someone sassed her, and now she thinks all of you are sassy. Maybe you did *nothing* wrong, but she's having a rough life.

For now, your teacher is an authority over you. You can try to win her—change her actions by doing what is right. Don't goof off in her class, and if your friends are giving her dirty looks or whispering, move away from them. Make an extra effort to be kind and helpful, even if you haven't been doing anything wrong. Try this for a few weeks and see if she lightens up. If not, talk with your parents about the situation. Maybe they will need to step in and help.

Is there a teacher you don't get along with?

What can you do to help the relationship be a little smoother?

Obey your leaders and be under their authority. . . . Obey them so that they will do this work with joy, not sadness. It will not help you to make their work hard.

Hebrews 13:17

4. Some of my friends start talking to me when I'm doing my work. So then I talk with them and get in trouble and don't get my work done on time.

Talking with friends is fun. When I was a kid, my report cards were mostly good. One year, though, almost every report card said, "Sandra would get much more work done if she wouldn't chat so much." It was embarrassing to bring that report card home, and it was embarrassing to have the teacher correct me in class. And yet it was so fun to talk that I had a hard time stopping.

Soon, though, the trouble it caused wasn't worth it anymore. It sounds like you're at that point. You don't get your work done on time, so you have to bring it home. You get corrected in front of everyone—even if you don't start the conversation. That can ruin a whole day—believe me, I know! Even worse than the trouble you cause yourself is the trouble you can cause other people by chatting in class. Your friends can't get their work done, either, and it's disrespectful to the teacher.

You and your friends can make a plan to chat during recess, free time, lunch, or after school. If you agree to concentrate only on your work during the study times, you'll have so much more time after school that the world will open up for you. One thing I did was keep a piece of paper on the top of my desk, and if I thought of something interesting I wanted to talk about with my friends, I'd jot it down. That way I wouldn't forget it by free time. It was always exciting to see what other people had written on their papers, too. It was almost like a game, looking forward to what my friends had written down to chat about later.

The main thing is, you're in school to learn, even though it's fun to talk. If you work hard, your knowledge will show it. You'll have something to be proud of! If you spend too much time chatting, knowledge (and your report card, like mine) will show that, too.

When do you talk in school when you're not supposed to?

What can you do about it?

Those who work hard make a profit.
But those who only talk will be poor.
Proverbs 14:23

5. It seems like I'm always behind, especially in math. What can I do?

Did you know that people learn in different ways? Some people learn best by hearing, some by reading, and some by doing. Besides that, researchers have found there are many different kinds of intelligence, or smarts. There is physical intelligence, which means you might do well in sports and with mechanical things. There is social intelligence (I think I had that—I talked a lot!). There is musical intelligence. There is artistic intelligence. And of course, there is intelligence with words and with numbers. There are as many different combinations of those skills as there are people!

The hard part is that schools focus a lot on math and on language. People, of course, learn these at different speeds. Even the very best of teachers can't guess the individual needs of twenty-five different kids at every hour of all days in each subject. They need to know that you're struggling in order to help you. You can be sure that everyone—parents and teachers alike—are eager to do just that.

God promises to give us wisdom when we ask Him for it. That doesn't mean that He promises to suddenly make you smart in, say, math when He's already created you with strengths in other places. But it does mean that He will show you what you need to do in order to finish your work. Perhaps that means He will help you find a tutor. Maybe it means He will give you understanding and you'll "get" something you didn't understand before. It might mean He gives you extra energy to study. It might mean that you need to learn some at home. I can't know how He will work, but I do know that when He promises something, He keeps His promise.

Ask Him for wisdom in how you can approach your schoolwork. Pray and ask, then listen for an answer. Let your teacher and your parents know about your struggles, too. The answer might come through them! I'll bet you'll learn a lot about how faithful He is when you see His answer at work in your life.

Which subject do you struggle with?

Pray and ask God for wisdom on how to approach the problem subject. What did He say?

But if any of you needs wisdom, you should ask God for it.
God is generous. He enjoys giving to all people,
so God will give you wisdom.

James 1:5

6. I want to go to a public school because I've never gone to one before. I'm homeschooled. I just want to try it for a year or something. But my parents don't want me to.

You might not believe this, but I get letters from kids in public and Christian schools who want to be homeschooled. I get letters from homeschooled kids who want to go to Christian or public schools. I get letters from kids in public schools who want to go to Christian schools. And so on.

Why? As they say, "The grass seems greener on the other side of the fence."

There are a lot of considerations a family makes when they choose schooling for their kids. Parents consider the strengths of the schools where they live, how much money they have, their job situations, and what kind of schools work best for them and their children. They think about how their child learns and what their child will be learning. Many times there are reasons for the choices your parents make that they haven't told you about.

Could you ask your parents to explain exactly why they chose to homeschool you? Be sure to ask for, and not demand, an explanation. This explanation is not for them to defend their decision, but to help you feel better about it. Then you can tell them what you feel you are missing—more friends, a locker, or whatever it is you wish you had by going to public school. Perhaps by brainstorming, your family can figure out how to solve your problem.

There is no perfect schooling option—Christian school, public school, and homeschool will each have some strong points and some weak points. But after prayer and discussion, you ultimately have to accept that your parents have selected with great love what they believe is best for both you and your family. Choose to be satisfied with their decision. Then settle back and enjoy the parts of schooling that make it special for you, your family, and your friends.

Do you wish you were schooled in a different way?

What do you feel you are missing? How could you get that in your current schooling situation?

I have learned to be satisfied with the things I have and with everything that happens.

Philippians 4:11b

7. I study for tests, but why don't I get an A?

When I was in college, I lived in a dorm room near a girl who always whizzed through her work. She never had to study and was always out having fun while I was back at the dorm studying, working, rewriting, and drinking coffee to stay awake! She got A's. I didn't.

One class, however, didn't come easy to her. I don't even remember what it was, but she tried to whiz through it like she had the others. She failed. She didn't study to learn how to do things or set her mind to hard work. Oh no. If she couldn't get an easy A, she just quit. No one respected her for that.

Now, some kids do study hard for their A's. They earn them! There is nothing wrong with that, and they—and you—can feel good when they get them. But you'll also find in life that hard work doesn't always bring rewards—the lead in the play, great grades, awards—right away. All that time you are learning to stick with jobs that don't come easily, you are quietly building the skills you'll need to be successful in life. And people *do* notice that! Later that year in college, my dorm advisor asked me to be on the Winter Carnival committee. She'd noticed I was up late studying and knew I would stick with the job and do it right. Work knowing that the One who sees all of your work will reward your effort some way, sometime.

Keep on learning. You are becoming wise and smart and building good habits. The way of life you develop by studying and doing what is right—no matter what grades you get—will repay you for a lifetime.

Have there been times when your work has gone unrewarded?

What are your two best study skills?

Don't get tired of doing what is good. Don't get discouraged and give up, for we will reap a harvest of blessing at the appropriate time.

Galatians 6:9 (NLT)

8. Sometimes people make fun of me because I seem to know a lot. What can I do?

Have you ever been in a neighborhood where every single house was exactly the same? Every house was the same style, with the same kind of roof, the same color paint, the same little patch of grass with one little tree in the yard. It's boring—and a little weird. Most neighborhoods have lots of different kinds of places to live. Big houses, small houses, apartments with pools, condos with shade trees, houses with tiny little windows on top to peek out of.

God made the human race like that. Some people (like me!) are shorter than most people. All people have different shades of skin. Everyone likes different styles of clothing. Most people think that is cool—God is very creative, after all. But some feel uncomfortable when people are different from them. They are threatened when they feel they are poorer or less pretty or less smart than someone else. Maybe that's why some kids are making fun of you. They think you are a threat to them.

When God blesses us with something, no matter what it is, it is not His intention for us to be too proud about it. God has blessed you with great intelligence. Make sure you are using it wisely—not showing off, not raising your hand every time you have an answer, not correcting others all the time. Don't compare grades. Try to ignore the people who are making fun of you, knowing that in their hearts they are feeling bad about themselves, not you! Then pray and ask God if there is someone you could use your smarts to help. You'll need to do this quietly, so as not to embarrass the person. Ask God how you could help this person, and then see what He answers. The Bible says people will see our good deeds and praise our Father in heaven. How can you use your smart brain—or anything else He has blessed you with—to bring glory to your Lord?

Who in your life could be blessed by something you have and they don't?

Check here after you pray and ask God how you can use this to glorify Him. ☐

Who is wise and understanding among you? Let him show it by his good life, by deeds done in the humility that comes from wisdom.

James 3:13 (NIV)

9. I'm worried there's going to be a shooting at my school.

I used to love reading the newspaper. I liked to see what was going on and read Dear Abby. But pretty soon I started noticing that all of the *head*lines were really *dead*lines—all about dying and death and bad things happening. People getting killed, robbed, or kidnapped were always up there in bold print. People helping others or enjoying life with their families were nowhere to be found—or else buried on the back page.

The fact of life is, bad news is scary, so bad news sells. Whenever something bad happens—like a plane crash—it's on the television hour after hour. Whenever something really fantastic happens, like thousands of people accepting Jesus Christ at a Luis Palau crusade, it barely makes a minute or two. So which do you think you hear more of, bad news or good? Bad, of course!

When we hear so much bad news, it can make us feel like the world is extra scary. And there *are* scary things happening around us from time to time, including school shootings. But there are many, many more wonderful things happening, like See You at the Pole, which happens at thousands of schools each year. Because we mostly hear the bad news, the world seems scarier than it really is.

No matter what's happening around you, scary or good, your heavenly Father is in charge. He does not take us out of the scary things in this world. In fact, He wants us to be the lights that shine brightly for Him during dark times. But He does promise us something even better: His peace. His peace is something we can't make ourselves have. It's something He gives us. When does He give it to us? After we give thanks. How does He give it to us? Through prayer.

Your Father doesn't want you to worry. He wants you to rest easy in Him. Try it and see how faithful He is.

What are you worried about right now?

Pray about it, right now. Okay. How do you feel?

Do not worry about anything. But pray and ask God for everything you need. And when you pray, always give thanks. And God's peace will keep your hearts and minds in Christ Jesus.

Philippians 4:6–7a

10. I'm afraid my grades will start to fall if I get one bad grade on a test, even though I'm a great student.

Aha! I'm not a doctor, but I'm diagnosing you with a common, hurtful condition. It's called perfectionism! My dictionary says a perfectionist is someone who has extremely high standards for herself and is unhappy with anything less. It also says it's a person who believes she can be perfect in this life. Such a person spends a lot of time being worried and unhappy. Why? We all make mistakes—we come in second or third or last place, or we do things we wish we hadn't done. Perfectionists are very sad and angry when those things happen. That makes them afraid a lot, because they are worried about looking bad.

Now, if anyone were to ask you, "Do you think you can be perfect?" you would answer, "Of course not!" In your mind, you know you can't be perfect. But in your heart, you expect yourself not to make mistakes. If you do make mistakes, you are really hard on yourself, right? You say things like "I should have known that," "Come on, that should have been easy," or "I'll do better next time."

The Bible tells us that we are to continue to grow in our faith and in Christlikeness. But it's also clear that we won't be perfect before heaven. In fact, once we realize that we *can't* do everything just right on our own, *then* we realize how much we need help! Does a perfect person—who does everything right, knows all the answers, and can save herself in every situation—show how much she needs God? No! But a person who knows she has weaknesses—that's a girl who knows she needs God.

When we tell God we can't do it on our own, we admit that we are weak. When we are weak, His power is made perfect in us. How? Because then we show others and ourselves the power of God at work. They know *we* can't do everything on our own, so we must be relying on Someone else. Then we give Him the glory, not keep it for ourselves. Sometimes when we want to have perfect grades or do everything just right, we really want people to admire us. Admit you aren't always the best and allow God to work through that. You'll worry less because you realize you don't have to be perfect. Why not? Because God knows exactly who you are and what you can and can't do, and He loves you just as you are.

What are some times when you are hard on yourself?

How could God's grace be at work in that situation?

But the Lord said to me, "My grace is enough for you. When you are weak, then my power is made perfect in you."

2 Corinthians 12:9a

Society

Do your part to live in peace with everyone,
as much as possible.
Romans 12:18 (NLT)

Quiz

YES NO

- ☐ ☐ **Do you ever wonder why so many people smoke?** *See page 92.*
- ☐ ☐ **Have you noticed that a lot of people lie?** *See page 93.*
- ☐ ☐ **Do you know what abortion is?** *See page 95.*
- ☐ ☐ **Does it bother you when people say that God did not create the world?** *See page 96.*
- ☐ ☐ **Do you ever feel different because of the clothes you are wearing?** *See page 98.*
- ☐ ☐ **Does it bother you when people do drugs?** *See page 99.*
- ☐ ☐ **Does it bother you when people don't take good care of the earth?** *See page 101.*
- ☐ ☐ **Are you upset that people are prejudiced?** *See page 102.*
- ☐ ☐ **Have you ever wondered why adults don't treat kids with more respect?** *See page 104.*
- ☐ ☐ **Do you ever wonder why there are so many mis sionaries but so many people still don't know God?** *See page 105.*

1. Why do so many people smoke?

When people start smoking, it feels good. It makes them feel light-headed in a fun kind of way. They think they look older. They think they fit in with the cool kids, kids they want to be like. Guess what? The good feeling doesn't last too long. Pretty soon smoking doesn't feel good, either. It feels very bad.

When you breathe, air goes into your lungs, and then your lungs send the air all through your body. When you smoke, it's like you are painting tar over those lungs. It gets harder to breathe. You cough up ugly brown stuff. Your skin gets wrinkled sooner and your nails crinkle. You smell bad. Not cool.

Most people don't expect to become addicted when they start smoking. Addicted means you have to keep doing something, even though you want to stop. Most adults who smoke want to stop, but they can't. It started out with them in control, but it's not long before cigarettes are in charge. People don't expect to end up with breathing holes poked through their necks so they can have oxygen tubes. But some do. People expect to be able to quit when they want. Most people can't. Many people who smoke die from lung diseases or early heart attacks. Almost all adults who smoke would tell you to run away from cigarettes, and that they'd do the same if they had a second chance.

Be cool—smell good, look good, and feel good. If someone offers you a cigarette, say, "No thanks." Then walk away.

Has anyone ever offered you a cigarette?

What will you answer when they do? Be prepared in advance!

Some people think they are doing what's right. But in the end it causes them to die.

Proverbs 16:25

2. What can you do when so many people lie?

Have you ever been about to get caught for something you've done wrong? Someone, maybe your mom or dad, asked if you'd done it. What was your answer? What were you tempted to answer? Lots of times we're tempted to answer, "I didn't do it," or even, "I don't know who did it." Those are lies, aren't they? Everyone has lied, even though we're ashamed to admit it. Why do people lie?

Most of the time people lie because they are going to get in trouble or because they want to seem more important. They are afraid of what's going to happen to them. Or they want to seem cooler or smarter or richer. But what really happens when we lie? The truth almost always comes out, and then we end up in much worse trouble than we started with. People don't trust or respect us anymore. Instead of keeping us from getting into trouble, it gets us into more trouble. We don't seem smart. Even if we don't get caught, we feel bad inside, knowing what we've done. If you know someone who lies a lot, you probably don't respect or trust that person anymore.

What can you do about other people's lies? If you know

them well, you can politely ask them if they are sure that is true. Mostly, though, you can be a good witness by your own honest talk. After all, each person must control her own mouth. The Bible says that every person will be responsible for the words they say. When we become Christians, we have the power of the Holy Spirit to do what is right. We are becoming more like the One who made us, and God never lies. Make sure that you tell the truth. Your honest words will be a great way to help others see how honorable it is to tell the truth.

When are you tempted to lie?

Is there someone you know who lies, whom you can be a good witness to?

Do not lie to each other. You have left your old sinful life and the things you did before. You have begun to live the new life. In your new life you are being made new. You are becoming like the One who made you.

Colossians 3:9–10a

3. What exactly is abortion?

There's a lot of talk today about abortion. It's in the papers and on the news, and people pray against it on Christian radio stations. If you haven't had a chance to talk with your mom or dad about abortion, this would be a good time to do it. Show them this page and tell them you've had this question, too. You can talk about it together.

Sometimes people make a baby when they haven't planned to. The people who made the baby might feel nervous or embarrassed about having the baby. They wonder how they will take care of the baby or how they will pay for it. If they don't have people to help them, they can feel afraid. One choice some people make when they are afraid is to stop the baby's life while the baby is still inside the mother. This is called abortion.

Whenever we stop someone else's life, it is wrong. God is the One who starts life, and it is God's responsibility to decide when someone's life will end. Whenever a person makes that choice, they are disobeying God. God has very strong words in the Bible for people who take away someone else's life, including the lives of babies.

Many people who've had abortions feel very sorry when they understand what they have done. They are sad and wish they had never done that. God forgives them, just like He forgives everyone else, including you and me, for our sins. The Bible says that if God is able to forgive people their sins, people need to forgive one another, too.

What questions do you have about abortion?

Have you talked with your parents about those questions? When will you?

You are the only Lord. . . . You give life to everything.

Nehemiah 9:6

4. When my teachers say that evolution is true and God is made up, I feel so discouraged.

Most people are proud of their independence. We say things like "I did it my way," "Rely on yourself," and "God helps those who help themselves" (which is *not* in the Bible, by the way). We're proud of the way we can do things on our own. When people are too proud of themselves, however, that pride is like poison to the soul.

Too much independence makes us think that we are in charge. We think we can make our own decisions without obeying or following anyone else. It means we don't have to answer to anyone. The only way *that* can be true is if there is no God. If we believe in God, we know He is bigger than we are. He is in charge. If someone wants to pretend to be in charge, she has to believe there is no God. Then she needs some other way to explain the beginning of the earth, the beginning of life. This is where the theory of evolution comes in. It's an explanation based on some true things around us so people do not have to believe God made the world. Some people believe God made the world and then it changed. That is a different kind of evolution from the theory that says God was not involved at all.

The book of Romans says that people know God because they can see His work all around them. But many people don't want to worship Him or give Him thanks, so they begin to think up foolish ideas. Then their minds are darkened to the truth. After that, they can't really see the truth anymore because they have already pushed the truth away from themselves. Keep peace in your heart during these discouraging moments, knowing that your eyes are opened to the truth and that God will protect you during these times. Work hard to have a respectable life. Then when you have the chance to speak the truth about creation or evolution—and you will—people will listen to your thoughts even though they may disagree.

Do you ever feel discouraged about the way the other people look at God's creation?

Whom can you ask to help you prepare a short answer about your beliefs?

From the time the world was created, people have seen the earth and sky and all that God made.

Romans 1:20a

5. Why is it that whenever I go out in public I have to look in fashion or people will make fun of me?

The clothes we wear say things about us. They can tell people which styles we like, if we are modest or not, and if we are daring or cautious. Outfits can sometimes show whether we've spent a lot of money buying them. People learn about us by what we are wearing before we even speak a word.

Why does that happen? Most people don't mean anything bad by learning about you through what you wear. After all, you choose your clothes, so your clothes give clues to who you are. People want to get to know you better, and one way to do that is just to look at you. They aren't judging you, they're just getting to know you.

But some people think they are better than others because of their clothes. They only like people who seem rich or cool because of what they wear. In the Bible, James 2:1–5 tells us that people who are nicer to those with better clothes or jewelry are making decisions using evil thoughts. Yes—evil! Pretty harsh, huh?

Next time you get dressed, realize that the clothes you put on say something about you. Is what you choose to wear saying something you want people to know? If so, then wear it with pride. Be confident that you are a whole person who expresses *some* of her personality through her clothing—but just a little. The people who know you best—or want to know you better—will find out much more as they spend time with the real you, inside your heart and mind. The ones who judge you based on your clothes aren't people you need to try to please anyway. Nothing you can do will please people who make decisions based only on what's on the outside.

Do you feel comfortable in the clothes you wear?

What could make you feel better about your clothing?

Never think that some people are more important than others.

James 2:1b

6. I don't get why people do drugs. It really bothers me. Why do they do that?

People start taking drugs for a lot of reasons. Sometimes they are pressured by their friends to try drugs to fit in or be cool. People don't want to lose their friends, so they try it. Often people who use drugs have problems at home or at school, and they think drugs will make them feel better. Sometimes people feel bad about themselves or think taking drugs will make them seem older or more interesting. What happens instead is that people lose respect for them. Good kids don't want to hang out with them anymore. No matter why people first try drugs, though, one thing is sure: Once they start taking drugs, it is very hard to stop.

This world is filled with both good and bad. Until we die, we will have sadness, trouble, anger, and disappointment. We choose how to deal with those emotions. We can try to smother them with drugs, but that doesn't solve the problems. It only adds more. Jesus says that in this world we will have trouble, but that we should be brave because He has overcome the world. Because we belong to Him, we don't have to depend on drugs for help. He will be our help.

The Bible says people are slaves to whatever controls them. If people have to take drugs to fit in, to forget about their problems, or to feel good about themselves, then drugs control them. They are slaves to drugs and need help to get free. If you know someone who is taking drugs, talk with your parents about it so they can help that person get free. And never take drugs yourself. A Christian should be a slave only to Jesus Christ.

What will you do when someone tempts you to try drugs?

What will you do when you know someone who takes drugs?

A person is a slave of anything that controls him.

2 Peter 2:19c

7. Why are people trashing the environment? Don't Christians care?

My family just moved to another state. While we were driving to our new home, we noticed thousands of blue and white garbage bags on the sides of the roads. Not just one road, but every highway we drove on. Sometimes there were ten bags stuffed with garbage and litter and junk every few feet. Dump truck after dump truck was loaded with this trash and, after emptying, came back for more. How did all this garbage get there? It mostly came from adults tossing it out of car windows. Who was picking it all up? The signs along the way said *Youth Ecology Working Here*. In other words, kids.

So often we take for granted the things we are given. What if you gave someone you love a birthday present and they trashed it—scribbled on it, got it dirty, let people spit on it? You would be hurt! You spent a lot of time planning for and picking out that gift, and you want it taken care of and appreciated.

The earth is a gift that God has given to us, and we are to take good care of it. Some people don't think about or believe that it was a gift. Maybe that's why they trash it. Just because the earth is important, though, doesn't mean it's as important as some people think. After all, the earth was not made in God's image. But people are. Still, we are to treat the earth with respect so that other people can enjoy it, too.

Be a good caretaker of God's good gifts. Don't litter in water or on the ground or even spit your gum out on the street. If you go hiking, walking, or biking and see some trash, pick it up. Spend a day each spring and fall cleaning up the area around your house or your favorite park. Encourage others to do the same. Christians, maybe even more than others, should treasure the gifts God has given them.

What things in the environment concern you?

What can you do about it in the next month?

The Lord God put the man in the garden of Eden to care for it and work it.

Genesis 2:15

8. Why does everyone have to be so prejudiced?

The word *prejudiced* means that people have prejudged you. They have made a decision about you without knowing very much about you. Maybe almost nothing at all! Normally when we talk about someone being prejudiced, we mean they have decided they are better than other people. Usually they feel they are superior to people of other skin colors, people who have less money than they do, people who are younger than they are, or even people who aren't good-looking.

Sometimes people are scared to talk with or get to know

people who are different from them. They are afraid that if they talk to someone with another skin color they will be rejected. They're afraid that if they are friends with someone younger, people will think they are babyish. But most of the time when people are prejudiced, they just like to pump themselves up by stepping on others.

The Bible never says that one skin color is better than another. In fact, it says that in Christ we are all equal. The Bible never favors richer people over poorer people—it's usually just the opposite! The Bible says that you must have faith like a child to enter the kingdom of God, so older is not always better than younger. The Bible also says that if we judge each other, we will be judged in the same way. Instead, we are to treat each other as brothers and sisters.

As Christians, we can show the world a better way by refusing to prejudge someone based on their outsides. Love others for who they are on the inside.

Whom are you prejudiced against?
(Be honest. It's just between you and God.)

How can you get to know that person, or that group of people, better?

So why do you judge your brother in Christ? And why do you think that you are better than he is? We will all stand before God, and he will judge us all.

Romans 14:10

9. Why don't adults treat us with more respect?

I know a twelve-year-old whose family was trying to figure out how to tie some bundles to the top of the car before a trip. She made a suggestion. Did anyone listen? Nope. They ignored her. Then they kept trying and failing with their own plans. Later, an uncle came out of the house and made a recommendation. He told them the exact same thing that the twelve-year-old had suggested. This time, because the idea came from an adult, they tried it. Guess what? It worked.

Sometimes adults are too busy to listen to kids. Sometimes they are too proud. That's sad, but true. Because of that, they don't always realize kids have a lot of wisdom and great ideas. If they did, they would respect you more. If you keep telling people your ideas, they will listen. The most important thing, though, is to prove to them that you are respectable and wise. How do you do that? The Bible says to be an example.

You have a lot of control over your life—more than you might realize! You can choose to speak with respect toward others, make good choices on your own, act with love, be faithful in hard times, and live righteously. So many people *don't* do this (both kids and adults) that even the most thick-headed adults will see the difference between your life and others. This will set a great example for them, earn their respect, and bring glory to your Father in heaven.

You are as important in the kingdom of heaven as other Christians of any age.

Are there times when you feel disrespected because you are young?

How can you set a good example for adults?

You are young, but do not let anyone treat you as if you were not important. Be an example to show the believers how they should live. Show them with your words, with the way you live, with your love, with your faith, and with your pure life.

1 Timothy 4:12

10. If there are so many missionaries, why are so many people still not saved?

You're right. There are thousands of missionaries in this world—actually, hundreds of thousands. A "missionary" is a person who has a mission. Their mission, or goal, is to tell people the Good News that Jesus died so that they may have eternal life. They also tell people they can have a better, more fulfilling and joyful life right now on earth if they live the way Jesus asks them to. Are all of these missionaries working in Africa or China? No! There are missionaries in almost all nations of the world, including the United States. Missionaries may move to somewhere far away, but sometimes people are missionaries in their own country. For example, there are Americans who are missionaries to Americans, and there are Korean missionaries reaching out to people in Korea.

Not everyone who hears the Good News decides to become a Christian. In the book of Joshua, chapter 24, Joshua tells the people that they must choose whom they will serve. Some people choose to serve God, but other people choose to serve idols or even themselves! You can't make someone decide to be a Christian. That is between them and God. But if they never hear the Good News, they won't even have the choice! That is where you and I and every missionary come in.

There are some people who are missionaries for their jobs. God led them to go somewhere and tell the Good News. Other people have regular jobs but are missionaries right in their own towns and neighborhoods. You can be a missionary, too. Just remember—it's your privilege to tell people and their choice how to respond.

Who in your life needs to hear the Good News?
(If you can't think of anyone, ask your mom or dad for suggestions.)

When can you tell that person about Jesus? Could that be your "mission" or goal?

"Anyone who calls on the name of the Lord will be saved." But how can they call on him to save them unless they believe in him? And how can they believe in him if they have never heard about him? And how can they hear about him unless someone tells them? . . . But not everyone welcomes the Good News.

Romans 10:13–14, 16a

Yourself

You made me and formed me with your hands.

Psalm 119:73a

Quiz

YES NO

☐ ☐ **Are you worried about getting your period?** *See page 110.*

☐ ☐ **Do you need help being a better athlete?** *See page 111.*

☐ ☐ **Do you still get angry at the things you've done in the past?** *See page 112.*

☐ ☐ **Are you having problems worrying about what people think of you?** *See page 114.*

☐ ☐ **Would you like to be a better example to others?** *See page 116.*

☐ ☐ **Is it hard for you when other kids are watching something on TV that you're not allowed to watch?** *See page 117.*

☐ ☐ **Do you criticize yourself a lot?** *See page 119.*

☐ ☐ **Are you dissatisfied with the way God made you look?** *See page 120.*

☐ ☐ **Would you like help making new friends?** *See page 122.*

☐ ☐ **Is everything about your body and mood changing, and would you like help dealing with that?** *See page 124.*

1. I feel really weird about getting my period. How old are you when you normally get it? Help!

As you grow older, it's normal to think about changes. Your body will change, beginning its path toward being a woman. Your emotions change. Everything feels funny and uncontrollable. Sometimes thinking about these things makes us happy—we're growing up! Yeah! Sometimes thinking about these things is scary. We're growing up. Uh-oh!

Each girl gets her period just as her body is ready for it, usually between the ages of ten and fourteen. When we begin to reach puberty, our bodies begin to change. Our breasts begin to bud; our baby fat melts off a bit; our skin becomes oily and breaks out. Soon we begin our period. Getting your period is a way your body reaches toward womanhood. It doesn't mean that you are a woman. No one expects you to act like a woman. It just means you're growing up in the way God intended for you. It can be an exciting time as you see your future begin to take shape before you.

Things won't seem so worrisome if you're prepared. Talk with your mom about what to expect. Get some supplies and keep some in your room, in your locker, and in a zippered pouch in your backpack. That way you won't be taken off guard. Some girls have light cramps once a month for a few months before their first period. They are aware that something is coming. Some girls are surprised when it just appears one day. Either is perfectly normal.

Look forward to growing up at just the right time. Being a girl is fun, but so is being a young lady.

What questions do you have about puberty?

Whom can you talk with about this? When?

There Is a right time for everything. Everything on earth has its special season.

Ecclesiastes 3:1

2. I need help being a better athlete. What can I do?

Our bodies are incredible. We can't even see most of the work that goes on inside. Our hearts pump about six thousand times every hour, more than one hundred thousand pumps each day. Our brains are faster and smarter than any computer yet invented. Our livers filter poison from anything we drink or eat. Dozens of other organs are at work. And all of this happens at the same time!

We may choose to push our bodies a bit to make them faster, stronger, or able to endure more. This is an important part of being an athlete. If you enjoy sports, you probably enjoy working out, too. Even if you don't enjoy sports, it's important to take good care of your body.

The Bible says that our bodies are the temples of the Holy Spirit. In the Bible, the temple was the place where God dwelled. God gave many pages of instruction on what His temple was to be like. People treated the temple with care and concern. You need to take great care of your body, too. It's the temple the Holy Spirit lives in now.

It's good to be the best you can be, whether it's in learning, character, or athletics. Train your body, practicing the moves you need for whatever sport you are trying to excel in. Ask a coach or a more experienced athlete what you can do to be better. Increase your workouts a little each week to build strength and endurance. But keep in mind that the time you spend working on your body will affect only this life. Make sure you leave enough time and energy to be with the Lord each day and serve Him well.

What can you do to be a better athlete?

How much time do you spend on spiritual training each day?

Training your body helps you in some ways, but serving God helps you in every way. Serving God brings you blessings in this life and in the future life, too.

1 Timothy 4:8

3. Sometimes I get angry about the stuff I did in the past.

Have you ever noticed that when you have a bad hair day you think everyone is staring at you? You probably feel really self-conscious. It can make you want to run home and stay there till your hair looks good again! In reality, it is most likely that nobody notices your hair except you. Why not? They're too busy worrying about their own problems! We all tend to focus on ourselves. That's not only true with outward things, like our hair and clothes, but also inside. When we make a mistake, or sin, we tend to focus on it a lot longer than anyone else does.

Jesus talks a lot about forgiveness. In fact, His entire life was forgiveness. He came to make a way for us to be forgiven. He wants to forgive our sins eternally, but He also wants to forgive our sins each day. That way we are made clean. The Bible calls this kind of clean "whiter than snow." Psalm 103:12 says that when God forgives us, He has "taken our sins away from us as far as the east is from west." How far is that? As far apart as you can get. He also tells us that when He forgives us our sins, He remembers them no more. He doesn't want them to stand in the way of our relationship with Him or with anyone else. He doesn't expect you to be sinless, and He doesn't want you to expect that, either.

If God can completely forgive your sins, can't you? If God remembers them no more, can you put them behind you, too? God does that because it's best for you, and He wants you to do that, too. The only one who wants you to be tormented by your past sins is Satan, because it will paralyze you from doing things today. If something is still troubling you, bring it before the Lord in prayer. Ask His forgiveness and the forgiveness of anyone else you might have hurt. Then move on, forgetting the past and reaching forward instead.

What have you done in the past that still troubles you?

What should you do about it right now?

But there is one thing I always do: I forget the things that are past. I try as hard as I can to reach the goal that is before me.

Philippians 3:13b

4. I'm having problems worrying about what people think about me.

Everyone wants people to think well of them. I remember when I was going to meet my husband's parents the first time when he was still my boyfriend. I dressed carefully. I took time with my hair. And then when I met his dad, I almost blurted out, "Hi, Big Bird!" instead of "Hi, Mr. Byrd." *Aaahh!* I was so worried I'd make a wrong impression I could barely speak straight.

The truth is, people will form ideas about you as they get

to know you better. They will learn what you are really like, and they have the choice to like you or not. But our value does *not* depend on what other people think of us. Our great value is in what God thinks of us. He thinks you are pretty special. He made you just as you are. He loves you, and Jesus died for you so you could be with Him forever. He must have thought you were okay to want to do that!

Guess what the best cure is for worrying about what other people will think? If you'll try it, I promise it will work. Every time you worry about what someone else thinks about you, change the subject in your brain. What do you change it to? Think of something kind or nice to do or say for the people you are with. Instead of focusing on *you*, focus on them. Ask how they are, what their day was like, if they want to do something together. Compliment them. Then do something together. Soon enough you'll find that you are loving others and not worrying so much about yourself.

In what situations do you worry too much about what others think of you?

What can you do about it?

Do you think I am trying to make people accept me? No! God is the One I am trying to please. Am I trying to please men? If I wanted to please men, I would not be a servant of Christ.

Galatians 1:10

5. No matter how hard I try to be a good example and shine so that my friends can see how much God has made a difference in my life, I just keep on doing bad things.

There's a word that Christians use sometimes, and it's a mouthful. It's called *sanctification*. It means becoming more and more like Jesus as you grow as a Christian. Of course, that means you are *not* just like Jesus when you first become a Christian. And you won't be sinless until after you die. So you're stuck in an imperfect world doing both bad and good things. How can you win?

The first thing is, the people around you know that you aren't perfect. Don't you hate it when someone is fakey and pretends that she has no problems? It makes you feel as if she's not being real. But when someone admits that she *does* have problems and is working on them, you respect her. The people around you, the ones you want to shine for, are watching you. They're not expecting you to be perfect. They want to see what happens when you're not.

Even the apostle Paul said, "I do not understand what I do. I do not do the good things I want to do. And I do the bad things I hate to do" (Romans 7:15). So what can you do? You keep trying. You pick yourself up and dust yourself off when you do something wrong. You apologize if you need to and ask God to forgive and help you. The next time, you'll be a little bit stronger, a little bit more in control. The fight against doing wrong things—evil itself—is a war. You can't win every battle, but you will win the war. Your friends will see you're not perfect, but that you're growing more like Jesus every day. *That* is something they can admire and copy. You shine more than you know.

What do you do after you sin?

Who is watching you to see how you respond?

Do not let evil defeat you. Defeat evil by doing good.

Romans 12:21

6. What if everyone is watching something on TV that you aren't supposed to, and you try hard not to, and kids are making fun of you because of it? What do you say?

It's never easy to be made fun of, especially when you

know you are doing the right thing. It's even harder if you are the only one who is going to speak up about not watching it. When you speak up, the others will think you are judging their TV shows. In a way, you are. You're saying that something they watch isn't good for them. This might make them defensive. When people are defensive, they are angry. You might be afraid of that. Or maybe you're afraid of being embarrassed because you're different.

If you're not supposed to watch those shows, it's either because your mom or dad has told you not to watch that particular program, or because there is stuff in it you know you're not supposed to see. Have you heard the saying, "Garbage in, garbage out"? People use that to talk about computers. If you type in a bunch of garbage, the computer will print out a bunch of garbage. That's what you put into its "brain," so that's what it processes. That's true about the human brain, too. Garbage in, garbage out. The problem is, garbage also infects your heart while it's in there. The damage lasts a lot longer.

If you don't want to make a big deal, just say, "I'm not allowed to watch this, and a TV show isn't worth getting in trouble about." Ask your friend to do something else. You might try leaving the room or concentrating on a book or something. If she keeps watching, you might suggest that you leave and come back another time. If people make fun of you, you can just tell them that you don't make the rules. You can tell them why your family decided that, or say nothing at all. You make the call.

What TV shows are you not allowed to watch?

Why does your family have this rule?

This is my prayer for you: . . . that you will see the difference between good and bad and choose the good.

Philippians 1:9–10a

7. I'm always criticizing myself and saying mean things about myself.

Are any of these sentences things you would say to your best friend?

> "That was stupid. You should know better by now."
> "I knew you'd look really dumb in that. You should have worn something else."
> "Every time you talk, people are staring at you because you make no sense."

I'll bet you would *never* say something like that to a friend—probably not even to an enemy! But those are the kinds of things we tell ourselves, inside, when we mess up or feel bad.

Self-talk is exactly what it sounds like—the words we say to ourselves. Sometimes we know we are talking to ourselves. Sometimes we have been doing it so long we don't even recognize it. The things you say to yourself will absolutely, positively change how you feel about *you*. If you tell yourself that you're dumb or stupid or ugly, it will make you feel more that way. If you cut yourself some slack—otherwise known as grace—you will feel better about yourself. When you feel better about yourself, you have some strength to keep trying, growing, and changing. If you feel bad, though, it makes you want to run and hide.

Next time you catch yourself saying something mean about yourself, stop. Ask, "Would I say this to my best friend? What would I say instead?" Be honest. You need to treat yourself with love, respect, and grace. Just like you treat others.

When do you say mean things about yourself?

What can you say instead?

Be humble and gentle. Be patient with each other, making allowance for each other's faults because of your love.

Ephesians 4:2 (NLT)

8. Sometimes I am dissatisfied with the way God made me

because I think my feet are too big. And I just got over my ears being *huge*. I am so tall, I have to stand with older boys in choir, and they call me Godzilla. It's embarrassing! Help!

Boys aren't always the most sensitive creatures, are they? Thankfully, they get better as they get older—trust me. But in the meantime, you still feel unhappy with the way you look!

Have you ever looked really closely at a baby? Usually we just look at them and think, *Oh, how cute*. Soft, fuzzy hair, darling little toothless grin. Next time you look at a baby, though, notice how large its head is compared with the rest of the body. It is much larger—the word is "disproportionate." It means that the body still has some catching up to do in order to be the right size to balance with the rest of the body.

Body parts don't all grow at the same rate. Heads grow large first, which is why babies have such large heads compared with their tiny bodies. Then torsos grow. As you have noticed, feet and hands grow faster sometimes, and then the body catches up. It can feel weird, but it is all normal. Your "big" feet aren't going to end up being too big at all. Your nice long legs are already catching up with them. Boys and girls don't grow at the same rate, either. Girls grow sooner, and usually stop growing sooner, than boys do. That makes girls bigger than a lot of boys for a while. Most of those boys who are teasing you are probably just jealous of your height! Soon the boys will begin to catch up, too, and most of them will grow taller than you.

Ask the Lord to help you see all of the wonderful and amazing ways He made you. Then hang tight for a few years till the boys catch up—and grow up. When you have finished growing, all of your parts will fit together exactly and perfectly, just as God has planned. You will be a completely balanced young lady.

Why are you dissatisfied with the way you look?

What parts of you are you happy with (pick at least two!)?

You made my whole being. You formed me in my mother's body. I praise you because you made me in an amazing and wonderful way. What you have done is wonderful. I know this very well.

Psalm 139:13–14

9. I'm really shy around people I don't know. And whenever I want to make friends with somebody, I either can't figure out what to say or I'm too shy.

It's hard for anyone to speak up. Even people who seem

much braver than you struggle with talking to other people, especially people they don't know. We might be worried that they won't accept us or that they will think we're weird. What if we don't know what to talk about? What if they reject us? It's especially hard when you want to make new friends. One thing I have learned: When life is especially hard, that is the time I must rely on God. And He is faithful to help me.

I just moved, so I left almost all of my friends behind. It's hard for adults to make new friends, too. I've found that I usually have to make the first move. So I pray and ask the Lord to help me. He knows that I need new friends. He is here to help me with everything I need. He knows I feel embarrassed and worried. But God also wants us to trust in Him and try to do the hard things. If you never try anything hard while trusting in God to help you, you'll never prove to yourself that He is there to help.

Remind yourself that it is normal to be shy—the apostle Paul even said he was much braver when writing letters and more shy in person. Ask the Lord to help you be strong and brave, to help you speak clearly, and to give you some good ideas about what to say. Ask Him to prepare a kind heart in the person you're going to speak with. Then go for it! The only way to have friends is to make friends, and you have to do at least half of the making! Don't give up if it doesn't go perfectly at first. Keep trying till you get to just the right new friend.

Whom would you like to talk with but have been too shy to speak to?

Pray right now, asking the Lord to tell you what to say and when.

On the day I called to you, you answered me.
You made me strong and brave.

Psalm 138:3

10. My whole body is changing, and my moods are, too! How can I prepare myself for these changes?

You are beginning one of many times in your life when you will have major changes. You are changing from a girl to a young woman. Your moods are changing because your hormones are shifting, whether you want them to or not! Your friends might be changing at the same time as you are. As you get older, your schoolwork and your responsibilities will vary, too. It can seem so out of control. But it's not.

You can't control the changes in your moods or your body, but you can change how you feel about them and how you react to them. You are a wise girl for even seeing that these changes are happening. That's the first step to controlling them! You can tell yourself, "I feel a little crabby today, but I can decide to talk to others more kindly anyway," "My body is changing, but I can control what clothes to wear," or "My face is changing, but I can control what cleansers and astringents to use." You have some control over how to respond to every change.

Life never stays the same; it always changes. If your happiness and security depends on things staying the same, you will be unhappy and unsure of yourself and life. Our security must come from God, who never changes. He is the same today as He was yesterday and will bc tomorrow. He is always good, always kind, always in control. He will be the same no matter what is happening around you. Hang your hope on that when the ride gets a little wild.

What changes are you worried about?

In what ways can you take control of those changes?

God does not change.

James 1:17c

And last but not least . . .

I have a question about something, but I didn't see it in Girl Talk. Where can I get an answer?

You can always ask your parents, your Sunday school teacher, or another godly person you know to help you look up an answer in the Bible. If you have a question that you think other girls would like to see asked and answered, too, you can write to me at the address below. I won't be able to answer individual questions, but who knows? It might show up in a new *Girl Talk* book!

Sandra Byrd
P.O. Box 1207
Maple Valley, WA 98038